English for Beginners.

The Book is divided into four parts to help you study.

Notes

Part One.

Contents.

<u>Notes</u>

Part Two:

Notes and Examples.

1) <u>Present Simple.</u>

    Facts.   I study English.

    Habits/Routines.   We pray five times a day.

    Certain Future Events.   They visit their grandparents on Friday.

    Adverbs of Frequency.   He sometimes plays the guitar.

2) <u>Spelling Rules for he/she/it present simple.</u>

    If the verbs ends in ch, sh, ss, o or x. add –es.

                              He catches, she washes, it misses,

                              he goes, she fixes.

    If the verbs ends in vowel and y.   add – s.

                              he plays, she stays, it enjoys.

    If the verb ends in consonant and y.   drop the y and add –ies.

                              He hurries, she worries, it carries.

    For the verb to be and to have.   he is, she is, it is.

                              he has, she has, it has.

3) <u>Present Continuous.</u>

    What is happening now.   We are studying English.

    The clothes you are wearing.   He is wearing blue jeans.

    Certain Future Events.   I am playing golf at the weekend.

4) <u>What are the spelling rules for present continuous?</u>

<u>If the verb is regular add –ing.</u>

working, drinking, eating, starting, doing.

<u>If the verb ends in e drop the e and add -ing.</u>

dancing, taking, hoping, having, writing.

<u>If the verb has one syllable and ends in one vowel and consonant double the consonant.</u>

stopping, planning, swimming, sitting, running.

<u>If the verb ends in double vowel and consonant don't double the consonant.</u>

sleeping, cooking, reading.

<u>If the verb ends in w, x or y add -ing.</u>

snowing, fixing, boxing, trying.

5) <u>When do we use have got?</u>

For possessions.   I have got a car.

For non-possessions.   She hasn't got a computer.

For illnesses.   He has got a broken leg.

For family members.   I have got two brothers and two sisters.

For features.   She has got blue eyes and long hair.

6)   <u>When do we use this, that, these and those.</u>

This for a singular item that is near.   This pencil.

That for a singular item that is far.   That book.

These for plural items that are near.   These chairs.

Those for plural items that are far.   Those tables.

7)   <u>When do we use capital letters?</u>

For the subject I.

To begin a sentence.

Days of the week, months of the year, public holidays.

Countries, nationalities, names of places.

People's names and titles.

Companies and Organisations.

Names of books, movies, songs and plays.

8)   <u>When do we use a, the and nothing?</u>

<u>a.</u>

Jobs.

Singulars.

Mention something for the first time.

<u>the.</u>

Mention something for the second time.

Rivers, Oceans and Seas.

V.I.P.s.

Superlatives.

Specifics.

Only one unique thing.

Countries classed as Unions and Republics.

Mountain Ranges.

<u>nothing.</u>

Names of people.

Names of streets and roads.

Names of towns and cities.

Names of continents.

Lakes.

General items.

Countries that are not classed as Unions and Republics.

Mountains on their own.

9) <u>What personal details will they ask for when filling out a form.</u>

Name.

Address.

Job.

Telephone Number.

Email address.

Nationality.

<u>10)</u> <u>What are the adverbs of frequency?</u>

always	usually	sometimes	occasionally	never
100%	75%	50%	25%	0%

11)   How do we tell the time?

What time is it?

Its' one o'clock.

Its five past one

Its ten past one.

Its quarter past one.

Its twenty past one.

Its twenty five past one.

Its half past one.

Its twenty five to two.

Its twenty to two.

Its quarter to two.

Its ten to two.

Its five to two.

Its two o'clock.

We use At and the time for when something happens.

The programme starts at eight o'clock.

The bus arrives at ten past six.

We use IT for what time is it now.

What time is it?

Its……………..

12)   One word question types.

When?   for time.
What?   for general.
Where?   for places.
Who?   for people.
Which?   for choice.
Why?   for reason.
How?   for the way you do something.

13)   Time prepositions.

On.

For days of the week.
Birthdays, dates.

At.

Exact Time.
Special Occasions.

In.

Months.
Years.
Times of day.
Seasons.

14) <u>When do we use and, so, but and because.</u>

<u>and</u>

<u>for additional information.</u>
We eat fish and chips.
I have tea and cakes in the afternoon.

<u>so</u>

<u>for the result of something.</u>
He was hungry so I made some dinner.
They were making a noise, so we told them off.

<u>but</u>

<u>for positive and negative situations.</u>
He would like to buy a new car, but he doesn't have the money.
She will visit on Monday, but she wants to visit on Tuesday.

<u>because</u>

<u>the reason we do something.</u>

I come to the British Council, because I want to improve my English.
He goes to the gym, because he has to lose weight.

15) <u>Nations and Nationalities.</u>

Sudan. Sudanese.   Britain.British.   America. American.   France. French.
Spain. Spanish.   Ireland. Irish.   Canada. Canadian.   Germany. German.

16)   Which sports do you play, do or go.

If a sport uses a ball we use play.

football, basketball, baseball, cricket, volleyball.

If a sport doesn't use a ball we use go.

swimming, skiing, cycling.

If a sport doesn't use a ball and is usually inside we use do.

gymnastics, karate, judo, yoga.

17)   Nouns and Adjectives.

A noun is the name of a place, a person or a thing.

A place is Sudan.

A person is Donald Trump.

A thing is a computer.

An adjective describes a noun.

Sudan is a   hot, dry, poor, big   country.
hot, dry, poor and big are adjectives describing country which is a noun.
Donald Trump is a   rich, famous, business   man.
rich, famous and business are adjectives describing man which is a noun.
It is a   new, expensive, nice   computer.
new, expensive and nice are adjectives describing computer which is a noun.

18) <u>Comparatives and Superlatives.</u>

Adjectives follow one of four rules in comparative and superlative form

<u>Rule One.</u>   <u>add-er, -est.</u>   young,
young,
younger,
the youngest.

<u>Rule Two.</u>   <u>add-ier, -iest.</u>   funny,
funnier,
the funniest.

<u>Rule Three.</u>   <u>more adjective, the most adjective.</u>   dangerous,
more dangerous,
the most dangerous.

<u>Rule Four.</u>   <u>irregular.</u>   good, better, the best.

bad, worse, the worst.

many, more, the most.

little, less, the least.

19) <u>Spelling Rules for Comparative and Superlative Adjectives.</u>

<u>Rule One.</u>   <u>If the adjective ends in e add r and st.</u>

large, larger, the largest.
strange, stranger, the strangest.

<u>Rule Two.</u>   <u>If the adjective ends in vowel and vowel don't double the last letter.</u>

deep, deeper, the deepest.
cheap, cheaper, the cheapest.

Rule Three.	If the adjective ends in consonant, vowel and consonant double the consonant.

big, bigger, the biggest.
thin, thinner, the thinnest.

Rule Four.	If the adjective ends in y and is one syllable drop the y and add ier and iest.

funny, funnier, the funniest.
crazy, crazier, the craziest.

Rule Five.	If the adjective ends in w don't double the final letter.

slow, slower, the slowest.
new, newer, the newest.

20)   Can you say twenty words in English without the letter a in them in ten seconds?

Yes, just count to twenty. The first number with a letter a in it is a hundred.

<u>Notes</u>

Notes

Part Three: Exercises.

One

Present Simple.

This is about you.

Put the present simple in the correct order.

There are twenty sentences to complete.

Present Simple Positive and Negative.

1   I/every day/get up.
2   I/teeth/brush/my.
3   I/shower/take/a.
4   I/work/for/ready/get.
5   I/office/an/in/work
6   I/eat/breakfast/don't.
7   I/tea/drink/coffee/and
8   I/morning/the/the/in/house/leave.
9   I/work/to/drive/don't.
10   I/bus/a/catch.
11   I/at/midday/lunch/have.
12   I/newspaper/read/don't/the
13   I/my/emails/check
14   I/work/again/in/afternoon/start/the.
15   I/evening/leave/in/the/work.
16   I/the/catch/bus/home.
17   I/home/arrive.
18   I/family/talk/to/my.
19   I/dinner/eat.
20   I/television/watch.

Part Three:

Exercises One

1	
2	
3	
4	
5	
6	
7	
8	
9	
10	
11	
12	
13	
14	
15	
16	
17	
18	
19	
20	

Two.

Present Simple..

This is about a family.

Put the present simple in the correct order.

There are twenty sentences to complete.

Present Simple Positive and Negative.

1. gets/in/morning/My/Father/up/the
2. He/work/office/doesn't/in/an
3. hospital/works/a/Doctor/in/He/as
4. the/house/leaves/He
5. doesn't/a/He/catch/bus/work/to
6. drives/He/hospital/the/to
7. Mother/housewife/is/a/My
8. breakfast/makes/She/the
9. Bruno/takes/my/brother/She/little/school/morning/in/the/to
10. My/comes/home/Mother
11. cleans/She/house/the
12. shopping/She/goes
13. food/buys/She
14. puts/it/in/car/the/She
15. She/home/drives
16. hurries/in/afternoon/She/to/school/the/meet/to/Bruno
17. brings/Bruno/She/home
18. dinner/eat/We
19. arrives/My/home/in/evening/the/Father
20. We/are/nice/family/a

Part Three:

Exercises Two

1	
2	
3	
4	
5	
6	
7	
8	
9	
10	
11	
12	
13	
14	
15	
16	
17	
18	
19	
20	

Three.

Present Continuous.

Tomoko is a Japanese student having an English Lesson at school.

This is about Tomoko.

There are eight sentences to put in the correct order.

Present Continuous Positive.

- is class the other students Tomoko sitting with in

- teacher listening are They the to

- studying English They are

- notebook reading is She her

- writing an exercise in She exercise is book her

- looking standing teacher The is everyone at and

- everyone listening have to going They exam so are an tomorrow is

- test the pass to hoping are They

1	
2	
3	
4	
5	
6	
7	
8	

Danielle is walking with her boyfriend Mark in the park.

This is about Danielle and Mark.

There are eight sentences to put in the correct order.

Present Continuous Positive.

- walking her boyfriend in the park Mark Danielle is with

- raining umbrella it is as holding They are an

- wearing trousers a coat is Danielle and

- jacket jeans blue wearing Mark a and is and

- going are what about talking are They do to weekend the at they

- cinema to the going are They

- restaurant eat dinner go to are going they Then, a to

- a have nice time going They are to

1	
2	
3	
4	
5	
6	
7	
8	

Dons United are losing.

This is about Dons United Football Team.

There are six sentences to put in the correct order.

Present Continuous Positive and Negative.

- a football season United Dons are having not good

- the at moment well playing not Egon losing are They 4-0 to City and they are

- singing not supporters The are

- leaving stadium are the They

- time good are They not having

- their club new for looking are They players join to new

1	
2	
3	
4	
5	
6	

<u>Four.</u>

<u>Spelling Rules for the Present Continuous.</u>

<u>Remember Present Continuous Spelling Rules.</u>

- If the verb is regular add –ing.

  working, drinking, eating, starting, doing.

- If the verb ends in e drop the e and add -ing.

  dancing, taking, hoping, having, writing.

- If the verb has one syllable and ends in one vowel and consonant double the consonant.

  stopping, planning, swimming, sitting, running.

- If the verb ends in double vowel and consonant don't double the consonant.

  sleeping, cooking, reading.

- If the verb ends in w, x or y add -ing.

  snowing, fixing, boxing, talking, trying.

<u>This is about my wife and I.</u>

<u>There are gaps to be filled in with the correct</u>

<u>present continuous verb to be and verb plus ing.</u>

<u>Present Continuous Positive and Negative.</u>

We_____to a restaurant tomorrow evening.

My wife Jane_____as it is her birthday.

I_____her out to dinner.

I_____as we_____ champagne with the meal.

We_____by taxi to the restaurant.

I _____her a very Happy Birthday.

are travelling   am taking   am not driving   am wishing

are going   are drinking   is not cooking

<u>Diana, Mark, Peter, James and John.</u>

Diana, Mark, Peter and James are a group called The Teddy Bears.

They are playing at a Hall this evening. Diana is the singer and she is driving to the Hall.

Mark plays the drums and he is taking a trumpet also. He sometimes plays the trumpet.

Peter plays the guitar and he is dancing also. James is going to play the piano.

James is not dancing because he is sitting at the piano.   They are going to play nice music.

Present Continuous Positive and Negative.

They_____at a Hall this evening.

Diana_____ to the Hall.

Mark _____ a trumpet also.

Peter_____also.

James_____ to play the piano.

James_____because he _____at the piano.

They_____ to play nice music.

There are gaps to be filled in with the correct present continuous verb to be and verb plus ing.

| is dancing | is not dancing | are going | is sitting |

| is taking | are playing music | is driving | is going |

Five.

When do we use have got?

My family and me.

Fill out the sentences below with have got or has got.(positive)

I _____ a computer and a bicycle.

I _____ a car.

I _____ a cold.

My Father _____ a cough.

I _____ four brothers.

She _____ long blond hair.

Fill out the sentences below with have not got.(negative)

Peter_____ a job.

Mark_____ a house.

Jane _____ a dog.

Lisa_____ a cat.

We_____ a radio.

They_____ a computer.

Six.

When do we use this, that, these and those?

Fill in the missing this, that, these and those in the Exercise below.

Exercise.

When do we use this, that, these and those?

_____ pencil here is mine.

_____ chairs here are for the teachers.

_____ tables over there are new.

_____ book near the board is for John.

Put in the correct word. This, that, these, those

Seven.

When do we use Capital Letters?

Read the sentences below and underline the incorrect parts of the sentences where there should be capital letters.

i am from burnley. it is a small town in the north of england. i lived there until i was 16. On tuesday i go shopping. i buy a lot of food and drink. my friend john sometimes comes with me.

january 1st is new years day. december 25th is christmas day. december 26th is boxing day.

barack obama is american. david beckham is english. pele is brazilian. maradona is argentinian.

mr john smith.   mrs frances davies.   dr. david taylor.   miss veronica jones.

the bbc make television programmes. the united nations send soldiers all over the world.

the united nations have an office in new york. the president of america lives in washington.

goldfinger is a book about james bond.

hard times is a book about difficult times in victorian england.

twelfth night is a play by william shakespeare.

titanic is a movie based on a true story.

Eight.

When do we use a, an and the.

Put in a/an or the in the missing spaces.

Fred is ___ fireman.

He wears___ uniform and works at__ _Fire Station in London.

Every day he drives ___car to work.

When he arrives, he parks___ car.

Then he puts on ___ fireman's uniform.

London is ___ biggest city in Britain.

Fred works at ___ largest fire station.

There are over 100 firemen working with him and he talks to ____ Fire Station Manager every day.

In the morning Fred, Adam and Dave and ____other firemen clean _____ Fire Station and look after everything.

When ____ fire is reported to ____ station _____ other fireman and Fred get into ____ Fire Engine.

Dave drives _____ Fire Engine and Adam tells Dave which way to go to _____ fire.

There was ____big fire on Warwick Street, London yesterday.

They work together at putting _____ fire out and it takes one hour to stop _____fire.

They drive back to _____ Fire Station.

They clean _____ Fire Engine and get ready again.

They write ____ report about ____fire and give ____ report to _____ Fire Station Manager who is in charge.

When he finishes work Fred drives home.

Fill in the missing spaces with a/an, the or X for nothing.

Buckingham Palace is in _____.

Glasgow is in _____Scotland.

He bought _____ nice shirt at _____ shop.

_____ supermarket is in _____ town centre.

James works in _____ bank. _____ bank is in _____ Manchester.

I have _____ car. _____ car is beautiful.

_____ cheetah is _____ fastest land animal.

_____ River Nile is _____ longest river in _____ world.

_____ food from _____ Italian restaurant is great.

_____ Paris is _____ capital city of _____ France.

I am staying with _____ friends.

He likes _____ fish and _____ meat.

_____ President of _____ U.S.A. is _____ Donald Trump.

David eats _____ apple and _____ orange for breakfast.

They don't like _____ sweets. They like _____ cake.

Work through the worksheet and then check your answers in the answer section at the back of the book.

Nine:

What personal details will they ask for when filling out a form?

You are booking into the Sea Front Hotel for an evening.

When you arrive the receptionist gives you a form and asks you to fill it out.

Your name is Mr. John Smith.

You live at 28 Moss Lane, Fulham, London. FE1 2HH.

You work as a journalist for a national newspaper.

Your Mobile Telephone Number is 0001-100000.

Your email address is JOHNSMITH1 @com

You are from Manchester. You are British.

Fill in the Details below.

Name:	
Address:	
Job:	
Telephone Number:	
Email Address:	
Nationality:	

You arrive at Dublin Airport in Ireland on a flight from London Airport in Britain.

When you arrive the Customs Officer gives you a form to fill out while he looks in your passport.

Fill in the Details below.

Name:	
Address:	
Job:	
Telephone Number:	
E-mail Address:	
Passport Number:	
Where was the Passport issued?	
What is the Passport's expiry date?	
Where are you going to stay in Ireland?	
Is your visit business or pleasure?	
When do you intend to leave Ireland?	
Do you have a return ticket?	

Your name is Joseph Ross.

You are a teacher and you live at 40 Moss Lane, Fairway, Manchester. M1 1KK.

Your phone number is 0111-111111 and you have a British Passport that was issued in Liverpool, England.

The passport number is ABC123000 and it expires on 01/10/2020.

You are staying at your Grandfather's at 22 Fallon Lane, Dublin. DA 1 2HP.

You have a return ticket to London booked for 31/08/2019 and it is 01/08/2019 today.

Ten.

What are adverbs of frequency?

Adverbs of Frequency usually go in-between subjects and verbs.

They explain how frequently we do something.

Adverb of Frequency.

Put in the missing adverbs of frequency.

They are always (100%), usually (75%), sometimes (50%), occasionally (25%) and never (0%).

I_____ play tennis at the weekend.   (100%)

You _____walk the dog in the evening.   (75%)

He/She/It_____ drinks coffee in the morning. (50%)

We _____ read a book.   (25%)

They_____ smoke.   (0%)

Adverb of Frequency Exercise One.

- They play tennis. (usually)

- He reads the newspaper. (occasionally)

- The girl reads. (always)

- The dog comes here. (always)

- They listen to the radio. (sometimes)

- They drink coffee. (never)

- It rains in England. (always)

- It snows in the Sahara Desert. (never)

- She cooks on Sundays. (always)

- I study English every day. (always)

Rewrite the sentences below in the correct order.

1
2
3
4
5
6
7
8
9
10

Adverb of Frequency Exercise Two.

Put the words into the correct order.

- I weekend the at usually clean bedroom my.

- We meat vegetarian never eat are we.

- sometimes I play Friday football on.

- occasionally come They and me visit.

- always bus at nine o'clock The arrives.

- usually David tea morning in the drinks.

- Francesca sometimes dinner cooks the Tuesdays on.

- never gym to the in Manchester Mike goes.

- Rose talks Mark to on telephone the always.

- The open on Christmas presents Day children always.

1	
2	
3	
4	
5	
6	
7	
8	
9	
10	

Eleven:

How do we tell the time?

When the long hand is between one and six it it past the last hour.

When the long hand is between 7 and 12 it is to the next hour.

What time is it?

It's...

Question.	Answer.
1)What time do you get up?	I get up at 8 O' Clock.
2)What time do you have a shower?	I have a shower at ten past eight.
3)What time do you go to work?	I go to work at half past eight.
4)What time do you start work?	I start work at five to nine.
5)What time do you drink coffee?	I drink coffee at ten past nine.
6)What time do you have lunch?	I have lunch at half past twelve.
7)What time do you finish work?	I finish work at five o'clock.
8)What time do you arrive home?	I arrive home at twenty past five.
9)What time do you eat dinner?	I eat dinner at ten past six.
10)What time do you watch television?	I watch television at a quarter past seven.
11)What time do you drink tea?	I drink tea at five past nine.
12)What time do you go to bed?	I go to bed at half past ten.

Draw in the correct times on page 38.

What time do you get up?

I get up at eight o'clock.

What time do you have a shower?

I have a shower at ten past eight.

What time do you go to work?

I go to work at half past eight.

What time do you start work?

I start work at five to nine.

What time do you drink coffee?

I drink coffee at ten past nine.

What time do you have lunch?

I have lunch at half past twelve.

What time do you finish work?

I finish work at five o'clock.

What time do you arrive home?

I arrive home at twenty five past five.

What time do you drink tea?

I drink tea at five past nine.

What time do you go to bed?

I go to bed at half past ten.

Twelve.

When do we use when, why, who, where, when, which and how questions?

Read about Fred Wilkinson the Fireman. Answer the questions using the present simple tense.

Fred Wilkinson the Fireman.

Mr. Fred Wilkinson works as a Fireman.

He gets up at 7.00 a.m. in the morning when he works during the day.

He gets up at 7.00 p.m. in the evening when he works during the night.

He travels to work by car.

He meets the other Fireman when they start work.

They clean the Fire Engines and look after the Fire Station.

When the alarm sounds they run into the Fire Engines.

They change into their fire clothes.

They arrive at the fire.

They put water on the fire to keep it under control.

When the fire finishes, they drive back to the Fire Station.

They write a report about the fire.

They clean the Fire Engines.

They finish work at 8.00 p.m.

Fred works two days from 8.00 a.m. until 8.00 p.m

Then he works two nights from 8.00 p.m. to 8.00 a.m.

Then he has four days off.

He likes his job

Question	Answer
What time does Fred get up?	
How does he travel to work?	
Do they clean the Fire Engines?	
What do they do when the fire alarm sounds?	
What do they do when they arrive at the fire?	
What time does he finish work?	
How many days does Fred work?	
How many evenings does Fred work?	
How many days off does he have?	
Does he like his job?	

Beryl and Brian the Bakers.

Beryl and Brian own a Bakers shop in a small town in Oxfordshire..

They get up at four o'clock in the morning to put the ovens on in the Bakery.

The Bakery is very near to their house so they walk to work.

Brian bakes all the bread and Beryl makes sandwiches and cakes.

They work together to get everything ready for when their shop opens at seven o'clock in the morning.

The customers arrive and they buy bread and cakes.

They talk to the customers.

At ten o'clock in the morning Brian puts some food into the Bakery van.

He delivers food to the local school, supermarket and offices in the town.

When he returns he helps Beryl prepare food for lunch time.

They serve lunch in the shop.

The shop closes at two o'clock in the afternoon.

They clean the kitchen and the bakery.

They walk home and they have dinner at five o'clock.

They watch television and they go to bed at half past seven because they get up early.

They work six days a week.

They have Sunday off.

They like their job.

Again, answer the questions using the present simple tense.

Question	Answer
Where do they live?	
What do they do?	
What time do they get up?	
Does Brian bake bread?	
What time does the shop open?	
Does Beryl deliver the food?	
Do they serve lunch in the shop?	
Do they walk home?	
Do they work every day?	
Do they like their jobs?	

Thirteen.

<u>We use on for days and dates. On.</u>

<u>Terry and Susan. They are husband and wife.</u>

I go to work on Mondays and I travel on the train.

I visit my Mother on Tuesdays and on Wednesdays I go shopping.

My wife and I play tennis on Thursdays and we finish work early on Fridays.

We drive the car to London on Saturdays. We watch a film and then we book into a hotel.

On Sundays we drive home and then we get ready for the next week.

<u>Days.</u>

What day does he go to work?	He goes to work on……………………………
What day does he visit his Mother?	
When do they finish work early?	
Where do they go on Saturdays?	
Where do they go on Sundays?	

Dates.

When is New Year's Day?	It is on……………………………………………
When is Americas Independence Day?	
When is Christmas Day?	
When is Boxing Day?	
When is your birthday?	

We use at for the exact time.

The Office Worker Dave.

I get up at 7.00 a.m. I have a shower and get ready for work.

I catch the 8.30 a.m. train. It arrives in Manchester at 9.00 a.m.

I start work at 9.30 a.m. I have one hour for lunch at 1.00 p.m.

I finish work at 6.00 p.m. I catch the train home and arrive back at 7.30 p.m.

I watch television and go to bed at 10.30 p.m.

Time.

When does Dave get up?	He gets up at...................................
When does he arrive in Manchester?	
When does he have lunch?	
When does he arrive home?	
When does he go to bed?	

We also use at for special occasions like Christmas and Eid.

Children at Christmas and at Eid.

Children open gifts at Christmas.
At Christmas children sing songs and play games.

At Eid people have a party. Parents give children money at Eid.

Special Occasions.

What do children do at Christmas?	They sing songs and play games.
What do people eat at Christmas?	
What do people do at Eid?	
Do people have a nice time?	

When do we use in for months, years and seasons. We use in the for the time of day.

The schoolboy Ryan.

In winter I wear a hat and coat. I catch the bus to school.

In November, December, January and February it is very cold. In the morning it rains and it is windy.

In summer I wear shorts and a T-Shirt. I walk to school.

In June, July and August it is very warm. In the morning it is hot and in the afternoon it is sunny.

In 2025, I am going to my new school. It is 5 miles from my house so I am going to get up very early and catch a train in the morning to arrive at the school in time.

Months, years, seasons and times of the day.

What does he wear in winter?	He wears a hat and a coat.
What is the weather like in December?	
What is the weather like in July?	
Where is he going in 2025?	

Fourteen.

When do we use and, because, but and so.

We use and for additional information.

I want fish and_____ please.

We eat fruit and_____ every day.

I have tea and_____ in the evening.

I sometimes eat bread and_____ with salad.

They serve coffee and_____ on a plane.

I need pen and_____ to write a note.

John and_____ are twins.

Dave and_____ are getting married next year.

France and_____ are in the European Union.

cakes	paper	Spain	vegetables	Anne
James	tea	butter	chips	

Put the nouns into the correct sentences.

We use because for the reason we do some thing?

I go to the gymnasium because……………………………………………………………

I drink tea because…………………………………………………………………………

We don't eat chocolate because ……………………………………………………………

They don't have a car because……………………………………………………………

He doesn't go to see them because…………………………………………………………

I drive a car because ………………………………………………………………………

He works as a teacher because……………………………………………………………

He doesn't play football because …………………………………………………………

You don't have a jacket because …………………………………………………………

You go swimming because …………………………………………………………………

he likes children	it is very hot.
it is bad for you.	they live in another country.
I want to get fit.	it is the best exercise in the water.
I like it	they don't have any money.
I like driving.	he hurt his leg.

When do we use but?

We use but for positive and negative reasons as to why or why not we can do something.

I want to buy a new car but I don't have any money.

1 He likes playing football but	
2 They eat steak but	
3 My Dad has a car but	

4 Jack plays tennis but	
5 Frank wants to see his Father this evening but	
6 Dave and Anne want to come and see us but	
7 They are welcome to come to the party but	
8 I want to see you but	
9 The cake is delicious but	
10 He is a nice man but	

Fill in the statements to match the sentences above.

the other people are not.	the sandwiches are terrible.
he doesn't play golf.	they don't eat fish.
they are not free next weekend.	he doesn't like watching it.
his wife isn't.	I am too busy at the moment.
he doesn't have a bicycle.	he has to work.

We use so for the reason why we do something?

I want to lose weight so I am going on a diet.

I need to improve my English so
We like dogs so
It is raining so
Harry is feeling ill so
Jane is tired so
We have an important exam next week so
He doesn't like his job so
She doesn't like the food at that restaurant so
The cat is beautiful so
My family like America so

he is looking for another one.	she is going to bed early tonight.
we are going to get one.	they are taking an umbrella with them.
we are going again next year.	we got one for my Father's birthday.
I have lessons.	he is going to see the Doctor tomorrow.
she is not going there again.	we have to study

Fifteen

Nations and Nationalities.

David a Police Officer.

David is from London, England. He is English.

He works as a Police Officer at London Airport.

He speaks English and French.

His wife is called Jane. She is from Ireland. She is Irish.

She works as a Secretary.

She speaks English, French and Spanish.

They are going to America on holiday next week.

Question	Answer
Where is Dave from?	
Where is Jane from?	
Does he speak Spanish?	
Does she speak French?	
Where are they going on holiday?	

Diane an Air Stewardess.

Diane is from Rome in Italy. She is Italian.

She works for an airline and she speaks Italian, German, French, Spanish and English.

She is flying to Madrid this afternoon from Rome.

In the evening she is flying back to Rome.

Her husband is called Joseph. He is from England. He is English.

Question.	Answer.
Where is Diane from?	
Is she Spanish?	
Where is she flying to in the evening?	
Does she speak German?	
Where is her husband from?	

.

Mark and Paul the Pilots.

Mark and Paul are Canadian.

They fly planes to America and Europe.

Mark speaks English and French.

Paul speaks English, French and Russian.

They are flying from Canada to France this evening.

The passengers on the plane are French, Canadian, English, German, Italian and Polish.

They fly an American plane.

They like their jobs.

Question.	**Answer.**
Where are Mark and Paul from?	
What languages does Mark speak?	
What languages does Paul speak?	
Where are their passengers from?	
Is the aeroplane Canadian?	
Is the aeroplane American?	
Are they flying to France this evening?	
Do they like their jobs?	

Sixteen

Which of these sports do you play, do or go.

If a sport uses a ball we use the verb to play.

If a sport doesn't use a ball we use the verb to go.

If a sport doesn't use a ball and is usually inside we use do.

Verb	Sport
	athletics
	basketball
	cricket
	diving
	fencing
	football
	gymnastics
	golf
	hockey
	horse riding
	ice skating
	judo
	karate
	lacrosse
	netball
	polo
	rugby
	running
	swimming
	squash
	tennis
	volleyball
	wrestling
	yatching
	yoga

Seventeen.

Adjectives describe places. Put the adjectives in the correct spaces.

Cairo is an _____ city.

There are lots of _____ buildings and it is the home of the _____ pyramids.

It is a very _____ and _____ city.   In the summer it is a very _____ place.

_____ tourists travel to Cairo every year.

hot	old	busy	international	Noisy	ancient	historic

Adjectives describe people. Put the adjectives in the correct spaces.

John is a _____ man.

He is a _____ person as he works as a Doctor.

He is a _____ worker as he works for twelve hours.

He is _____ and _____.

This is what you need to be a _____ Doctor.

hard	kind	nice	good	helpful	clever

Adjectives describe things.   Put the adjectives in the correct spaces.

I have a _____ computer.

It is _____ and _____.

It is an _____ computer.

expensive	new	Fantastic	nice

Eighteen.

Comparative and Superlative Adjectives.

Rule One.

For some comparative and superlatives we add -er and -est.

tall

old

young

small

kind

tall.

The Empire State is a _____ building.

The Sears Tower is _____ than the Empire State.

The Burja Khalifa is the _____ building in the world.

old.

Rome is an _____ city.

Athens is _____ than Rome.

Luxor is the _____ city in the world.

young.

A child is a _____ person.

A infant is _____ than a child.

A baby is the _____.

small.

A cat is a _____ animal.

A mouse is _____ than a cat.

An insect is the _____ .

kind.

Peter a _____ man.

Tony is _____ than Peter.

Dennis is the _____ man.

We add -er and -est to these adjectives.

Remember Comparatives compare two sets of things and Superlative look at three sets of things.

Rule Two.

If adjective ends in y we drop the y and add -ier and -iest.

funny

lazy

busy

noisy

happy

funny

Jimmy is a _____ man.

John is _____ than Jimmy.

Gerry is the _____ person in the family.

<u>lazy.</u>

Andy is a _____ man.

Chris is _____ than Andy.

Eddie is the _____ person in the group.

<u>busy.</u>

Manchester is a _____ city.

London is _____ than Manchester.

Tokyo is the _____ city in the world.

<u>noisy.</u>

Delhi is a _____ city.

Paris is _____ than Delhi.

Cairo is the _____ city in the world.

<u>happy.</u>

Adele is a _____ child.

Melanie is _____ than Adele.

Alison is the _____ person in the group.

<u>This rule also applies to adjectives like crazy, dirty and easy.</u>

Rule Three.

Some adjectives follow more with the adjective and the most with the adjective.

beautiful

dangerous

expensive

important

responsible

beautiful.

A Ford is a	car.
A Porsche is more	than a Ford.
A Rolls Royce is the	car.

Dangerous.

Polar Bears are	animals.
Snakes are more	than Polar Bears.
Lions are the	dangerous animals.

expensive.

It is an	silver ring.
The gold ring is	than the silver ring.
The Diamonds are	most expensive things.

important.

A private is an	soldier.
An officer is	than a soldier.
A General is the	soldier.

responsible.

A teacher is a _____ person.

A senior teacher is _____ than a teacher.

A Headteacher is the _____ person in a school.

Remember for this rule we use more _____ adjective

most _____ adjective.

Rule Four

Irregular Adjectives.

A few adjectives do not follow these rules.

They are good, bad, many and little.

good	better	the best
bad	worse	the worst
many	more	the most.
little	less	the least.

Good

David is a _____ footballer.

Mark is a _____ than David.

Peter is the _____ footballer on the team.

Bad

It is _____ weather today in England.

In Scotland it is _____ than England.

Ireland has the _____ worst weather today.

Many

There are _____ tables in the class.

There are _____ tables in the next class.

There are the _____ tables in the storeroom.

Little.

There is a _____ petrol in my car.

There is _____ petrol in Dave's car.

There is the _____ petrol in Mark's car.

Nineteen.

What are the spelling rules for Comparative and Superlative Adjectives?

Rule One.

If the adjective ends in e and is one syllable add r and st.

      large, larger, the largest.

      safe, safer, the safest.

      strange, stranger, the strangest.

      wise, wiser, the wisest.

Wise.

      A dolphin a _____ animal.
      An elephant is_____than a dolphin.
      An owl is the_____animal.

Rule Two.

If the adjective ends is vowel and vowel we don't double the last letter.

deep, deeper, the deepest.

steep, steeper, the steepest.

cheap, cheaper, the cheapest.

Deep   It is a_____river.

The sea is_____ than the river.

The ocean is the_____.

Rule Three.

If the adjective ends in consonant, vowel and consonant double the last consonant.

big, bigger, the biggest.

fat, fatter, the fattest.

thin, thinner, the thinnest.

slim, slimmer, the slimmest.

tall, taller, the tallest.

hot, hotter, the hottest.

Hot   Spain is a_____country.

India is_____ than Spain.

The Sahara is the_____ place on earth.

Rule Four.

If the adjective ends in y and drop the y and add ier and iest.

funny, funnier, the funniest.

crazy, crazier, the craziest.

lazy, lazier, the laziest.

noisy, noisier, the noisiest.

dirty, dirtier, the dirtiest.

Lazy John is a _____man.

Jane is _____than John.

Kevin is the _____person in the group.

Rule Five.

If the adjective ends in w don't double the final letter.

slow, slower, the slowest.

new, newer, the newest.

New He has a _____computer.

She has a _____computer.

I have the _____computer.

Notes

Notes

Part Four: **Answers.**

One.

This is about you.

I

Present Simple.

I get up every day. I brush my teeth and then I take a shower. I get ready for work.

I work in an office. I don't eat breakfast but I drink tea and coffee.

I leave the house in the morning. I don't drive to work. I catch a bus.

I have lunch at midday. I don't read the newspaper but I check my emails.

I start work again in the afternoon. I leave work in the evening and I catch the bus home.

I arrive home and I talk to my family. I eat dinner and I watch television.

Conversation Building.

Tell you partner five things you do every day.

I get up.

I watch television.

I go to school.

I check my emails.

I clean my teeth.

Tell your partner five things you don't do every day.

I don't play football.

I don't ride a bicycle.

I don't drink tea.

I don't telephone my friends.

I don't drive a car.

Then listen to five things that you partner does or does not do.

When you ask the questions remember the structure.

Do you play tennis?   Yes, I do. / No, I don't.

Do you read books?

Do you use a computer?

Do you eat fish?

Do you drink coke?

Do/present form of the verb/object?   Yes, subject do. No, subject don't

Two.

This is about third person.

He/She/It

Present Simple.

This is about a Family.

My Father gets up in the morning. My Father doesn't work in an office.

He works as a Doctor in a hospital. He leaves the house. He doesn't catch a bus to work.

He drives to the hospital.

My Mother is a housewife. She makes the breakfast and she takes my little brother Bruno to school in the morning. My Mother comes home and she cleans the house. Then, she goes shopping.

She buys food and she puts it in the car. Then, she drives home.

In the afternoon she hurries to school to meet Bruno. She brings Bruno home and we eat dinner when my Father arrives home in the evening. We are a nice family.

Conversation Building.

Tell your friend five things your Father, Mother, Brother, Sister or Friend do every day.

Yes, he/she does.

No, he she doesn't.

Does he/she play tennis?

Does he/she watch television?

Does he/she read a book?

Does he/she go to work?

Does he/she drink orange juice?

Three.

Present Continuous.

Tomoko is a Japanese student having an English Lesson at school.

Tomoko is sitting in class with the other students. They are listening to the teacher. They are studying English. She is reading her notebook. She is writing in her exercise book. The teacher is standing and looking at everyone. They are going to have an exam tomorrow so everyone is listening. They are hoping to pass the test.

Danielle is walking with her boyfriend Mark in the park.

Danielle is walking with her boyfriend Mark in the park. They are holding an umbrella as it is raining. Danielle is wearing a coat and trousers. Mark is wearing blue jeans and a jacket. They are talking about what they are going to do at the weekend. They are going to the cinema. Then, they are going to go to a restaurant to eat dinner. They are going to have a nice time.

The Dons United are losing.

Dons United are not having a good football season.

They are losing to Egon City 4-0 at the moment and they are not playing well.

The supporters are not singing. They are leaving the stadium.

They are not having a good time.

They are looking for new players to join their club.

Conversation Building.

Question	Answer
Question	**Answer**
You.	
Are you playing football?	Yes, I am, /No, I am not.
Your Father/Husband/Brother/Friend.	
Is he watching television?	Yes, he is/No, he is not.
Your Mother/Wife/Sister/Friend.	
Is she reading a book?	Yes, she is/No, she is not.
Your friends.	
Are they drinking coffee?	Yes, they are. / No, they are not.
Present of the verb to be/subject/verb+ing?	Yes, subject verb to be.
	No, subject verb to be.

This question can be for any present continuous action happening now, in the future or for the clothes you are wearing.

Ask and answer as many examples as possible with you friends.

Four.

Spelling Rules for the Present Continuous.

My wife and I.

We are going to a restaurant tomorrow evening.

My wife Jane is not cooking as it is her birthday.

I am taking her out to dinner.

I am not driving as we are drinking champagne with the meal.

We are travelling by taxi to the restaurant.

I am wishing her a very Happy Birthday.

Diana, Mark, Peter and James.

Diana, Mark, Peter and James are a group called The Teddy Bears.

They are playing at a Hall this evening. Diana is the singer and she is driving to the Hall.

Mark plays the drums and he is taking a trumpet also. He sometimes plays the trumpet.

Peter plays the guitar and he is dancing also. James is going to play the piano.

James is not dancing because he is sitting at the piano.   They are going to play nice music.

Five.

When do we use have got?   Answers to the section.

My family and I.

I have got a computer and a bicycle. I have not got a car.

I have got a cold. My Father has got a cough.

I have got four brothers.

My Mother is very beautiful. She has got long blond hair.

My Brother.

He has got a nice flat. He has got grey hair. He has got a nice blue suit.

He has got one daughter. He has got one brother and two sisters.

They have got families of their own.

He has not got a bicycle but he has got a car.

My Mother and Father.

They have got a nice house. It has got four bedrooms. It has got a lovely garden.

They have got two sons and two daughters. They have got five grandchildren.

They have not got any animals. They have not got a car.

My Father has got brown hair and blue eyes.

My family and I.(2)

Fill out the sentences below with have got or has got.(positive)

I have got a computer and a bicycle.

I have got a car.

I have got a cold.

My Father has got a cough.

I have got two brothers.

She has got long blond hair.

Fill out the sentences below with have not got.(negative)

Peter has not got a job.

Mark has not got a house.

Jane has not got a dog.

Lisa has not got a cat.

We have not got a radio.

They have not got a computer.

Conversation Building.

Question.	**Answer.**	
Have you got a brother?	Yes, I have.	No, I have not.
Has he got a cold?	Yes, he has.	No, he has not.
Has she got blue eyes?	Yes, she has.	No, she has not.
Has the car got a heater?	Yes, it has.	No, it has not.
Have we got a computer?	Yes, we have.	No, we have not.
Have they got a pen?	Yes, they have.	No, they have not.

<u>Six.</u>

<u>When do we use this, that, these and those?</u>

This pencil here is mine.

These chairs here are for the teachers.

Those tables over there are new.

That book near the board is for John.

<u>Seven.</u>

I am from Burnley. It is a small town in the north of England. I lived there until I was 16.

On Tuesday I go shopping. I buy a lot of food and drink. My friend John sometimes comes with me.

January 1st is New Year's Day. December 25th is Christmas Day. December 26th is Boxing Day.

Barack Obama is American. David Beckham is English. Pele is Brazilian. Maradona is Argentinian.

Mr. John Smith.   Mrs Frances Davies.   Dr. David Taylor.   Miss Veronica Jones.

The B.B.C. make television programmes. The United Nations send soldiers all over the world.

The United Nations have an office in New York. The President of America lives in Washington.

Goldfinger is a book about James Bond.
Hard Times is a book about Victorian England.

Twelfth Night is a play by William Shakespeare.

Titanic is a movie based on a true story.

<u>Eight.</u>

<u>When do we use a, an and the.</u>

<u>Put in a/an or the in the missing spaces.</u>

Fred is a fireman.

He wears a uniform and works at a Fire Station in London.

Every day he drives a car to work.

When he arrives, he parks the car.

Then he puts on a fireman's uniform.

London is the biggest city in Britain.

Fred works at the largest fire station.

There are over 100 firemen working with him and he talks to the Fire Station Manager every day.

In the morning Fred, Adam and Dave and the other firemen clean the Fire Station and look after everything.

When a fire is reported to the station the other fireman and Fred get into a Fire Engine.

Dave drives the Fire Engine and Adam tells Dave which way to go to the fire.

There was a big fire on Warwick Street, London yesterday.

They work together at putting the fire out and it takes one hour to stop the fire.

They drive back to the Fire Station.

They clean the Fire Engine and get ready again.

They write a report about the fire and give the report to the Fire Station Manager who is in charge.

When he finishes work Fred drives home.

<u>Put in a/an or the in the missing spaces.</u>

Nine:

Filling in Personal Details.

Your name is Mr. John Smith.

You live at 28 Moss Lane, Fulham, London. FE1 2HH.

You work as a journalist for a national newspaper.

Your Mobile Telephone Number is 0001-100000.

Your email address is JOHNSMITH1 @com

You are from Manchester. You are British.

Fill in the Details below.

Name:	Mr. John Smith.
Address:	28 Moss Lane, Fulham, London. FE1 2HH.
Job:	Journalist.
Telephone Number:	0001-100000
Email Address:	JOHNSMITH1@com
Nationality:	British

You arrive at Dublin Airport in Ireland on a flight from London Airport in Britain.

When you arrive the Customs Officer gives you a form to fill out while he looks in your

passport.

Fill in the Details below.

Name:	Joseph Ross
Address:	40 Moss Lane, Fairway, Manchester. M1 1KK.
Job:	Teacher.
Telephone Number:	01111-111111
E-mail Address:	ross1@gmail
Passport Number:	ABC123000
Where was the Passport issued?	Liverpool, England
What is the Passport's expiry date?	01/10/2019
Where are you going to stay in Ireland?	22 Fallon Lane, Dublin. DA1 2HP.
Is your visit business or pleasure?	Pleasure.
When do you intend to leave Ireland?	On 31/08/2019
Do you have a return ticket?	Yes.

Your name is Joseph Ross.

You are a teacher and you live at 40 Moss Lane, Fairway, Manchester. M1 1KK.

Your phone number is 0111-111111 and you have a British Passport that was issued in Liverpool, England.

Your email address is ross1@gmail

The passport number is ABC123000 and it expires on 01/10/2030.

You are staying at your Grandfather's at 22 Fallon Lane, Dublin. DA 1 2HP.

You have a return ticket to London booked for 31/08/2019 and it is 01/08/2019 today.

Conversation Building Exercise.

Questions and Answers at an airport, a Doctor's, a hospital, a hotel, an interview.etc.

Question.	**Answer.**
What is your full name?	My name is …………………………………..
How do you spell your family name?	S M I T H
What is your address?	It is…………………………………………..
What is your telephone number?	It is………………………………………….
What is your email address?	It is………………………………………….
What is your job?	I am a…………………………………….……
What is your passport number?	It is………………………………………….
When does the passport expire?	It expires on……………………………….

Ten.

Adverb of Frequency.   Put in the missing adverbs of frequency.

They are always (100%), usually (75%), sometimes (50%), occasionally (25%) and never (0%).

I	always	play tennis at the weekend.	(100%)
You	usually	walk the dog in the evening.	(75%)
He/She/It	sometimes	drinks coffee in the morning.	(50%)
We	occasionally	read a book.	(25%)
They	never	smoke.	(0%)
subject	adverb of frequency	verb	

Adverb of Frequency Exercise One.

Answers to the Exercise in Section Four.

Rewrite the sentences below in the correct order.

1	They usually play tennis
2	He occasionally reads the newspaper.
3	The girl always reads.
4	The dog always comes here.
5	They sometimes listen to the radio.
6	They never drink coffee.
7	It always rains in England.
8	It never snows in the Sahara Desert.
9	She always cooks on Sundays.
10	I always study English every day.

Adverb of Frequency Exercise Two.

Answers to the Exercise in Section Four.

1	I usually clean my bedroom at the weekend.
2	We never eat meat. We are vegetarian.
3	I sometimes play football on Friday.
4	They occasionally visit me.
5	The bus always arrives at nine o'clock.
6	David usually drinks tea in the morning.
7	Francesca sometimes cooks the dinner on Tuesdays.
8	Mike never goes to the gym in Manchester.
9	Rose always talks to Mark on the telephone.
10	The children always open presents on Christmas Day.

Conversation Building Exercise.

Adverb of Frequency Questions.

Questions.

For your Mother/Father./Brother/Sister/Friend

Do you always text your friends?   Does she/he always wash the dishes?

Do you usually eat breakfast?   Does she/he usually read a book?

Do you sometimes drink milk?   Does she/he sometimes play golf?

Do you occasionally play the guitar?   Does she/he occasionally watch football?

Do you ever smoke a cigarette?   Does she/he ever drink beer?

Do you always study English?   Does she/he always work in an office?

Do you usually listen to music?   Does she/he usually talk to you?

Do you sometimes watch the television?   Does she/he sometimes use the computer?

Do you occasionally play football?   Does she/he occasionally drive a car?

Do you ever ride a bicycle?   Does she/he ever go on holiday?

Do/subject/adverb of frequency/verb?   Does/she/he/it/adverb of frequency/verb?

Answers.   ## Answers.

Yes, I do.   Yes, she/he does.

No, I don't.   No, she/he doesn't.

Eleven.

Telling the time.
Draw the time on the twelve clocks below.
The clocks with the drawn in corrected times.
What time do you get up?
I get up at eight o'clock.
What time do you have a shower?
I have a shower at ten past eight.
What time do you go to work?
I go to work at half past eight.
What time do you start work?
I start work at five to nine.
What time do you drink coffee?
I drink coffee at ten past nine.
What time do you have lunch?
I have lunch at half past twelve.
What time do you finish work?
I finish work at five o'clock.
What time do you arrive home?
I arrive home at twenty past five.
What time do you drink tea?
I drink tea at five past nine.
What time do you go to bed?
I go to bed at half past ten.

Answers

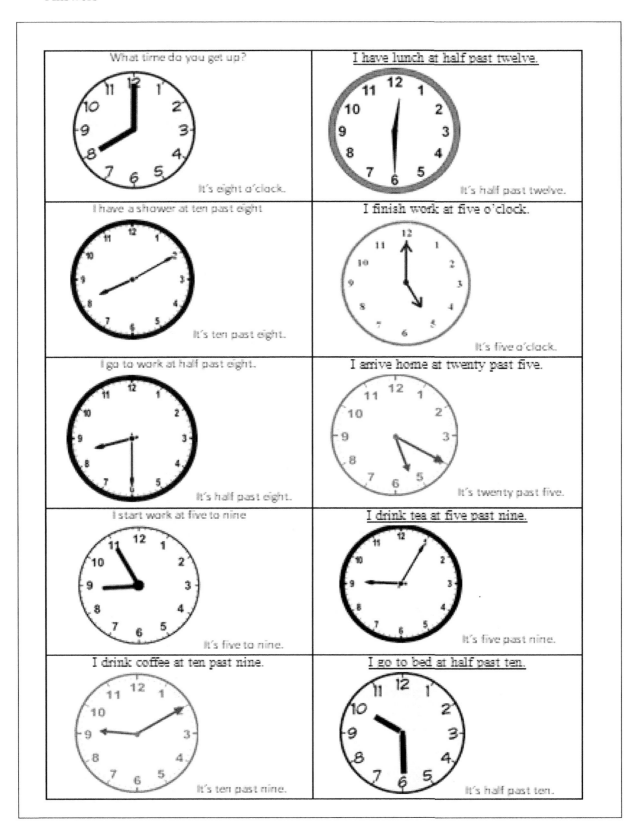

What time do you get up?	I have lunch at half past twelve.
It's eight o'clock.	It's half past twelve.
I have a shower at ten past eight	I finish work at five o'clock.
It's ten past eight.	It's five o'clock.
I go to work at half past eight.	I arrive home at twenty past five.
It's half past eight.	It's twenty past five.
I start work at five to nine	I drink tea at five past nine.
It's five to nine.	It's five past nine.
I drink coffee at ten past nine.	I go to bed at half past ten.
It's ten past nine.	It's half past ten.

Conversation Building Exercise.

Question.	Positive.

What time do you get up?   I get up at……………………….,………….

What time do you eat breakfast?

What time do you go to work?

What time do you eat lunch?   Negative.

What time do you drink coffee?   I don't drink coffee. I drink tea at ten o'clock.

What time do you go home?

What time do you eat dinner?

What time do you watch television?

Question.	Positive.

What time does he/she get up?   He/ She gets up at…………………….,………..

What time does he/she eat breakfast?

What time does he/she go to work?

What time does he/she eat lunch?   Negative.

What time does he/she drink coffee? He does not drink coffee. He drinks tea at ten o'clock.

What time does he/she go home?

What time does he/she eat dinner?

What time does he/she watch television?

Twelve./When do we use when, why, who, where, when, which and how questions?

Read the section below about: Fred Wilkinson the Fireman.

Fred Wilkinson the Fireman.

Mr. Fred Wilkinson works as a Fireman.

He gets up at 7.00 a.m. in the morning when he works during the day.

He gets up at 7.00 p.m. in the evening when he works during the night.

He travels to work by car.

He meets the other Fireman when they start work.

They clean the Fire Engines and look after the Fire Station.

When the alarm sounds they run into the Fire Engines.

They change into their fire clothes.

They arrive at the fire.

They put water on the fire to keep it under control.

When the fire finishes, they drive back to the Fire Station.

They write a report about the fire.

They clean the Fire Engines.

They finish work at 8.00 p.m.

Fred works two days from 8.00 a.m. until 8.00 p.m

Then he works two nights from 8.00 p.m. to 8.00 a.m.

Then he has four days off. He likes his job.

Question.	Answer.
What time does Fred get up?	He gets up at 7.00 a.m. in the morning. He gets up at 7.00 p.m. in the evening.
How does he travel to work?	He travels to work by car.
Do they clean the Fire Engines?	Yes, they do.
What do they do when the fire alarm sounds?	They get in the Fire Engines. They drive to the Fire.
What do they do when they arrive at the fire?	They put water on the fire. They put the fire out.
What time does he finish work?	He finishes work at 8.00 a.m. in the morning. He finishes work at 8.00 p.m. in the evening.
How many days does Fred work?	He works for two days.
How many evenings does Fred work?	He works for two evenings.
How many days off does he have?	He has four days off.
Does he like his job?	Yes, he does.

Beryl and Brian the Bakers.

Beryl and Brian own a Bakers shop in a small town in Oxfordshire..

They get up at four o'clock in the morning to put the ovens on in the Bakery.

The Bakery is very near to their house so they walk to work.

Brian bakes all the bread and Beryl makes sandwiches and cakes.

They work together to get everything ready for when their shop opens at seven o'clock in the

morning.

The customers arrive and they buy bread and cakes.

They talk to the customers.

At ten o'clock in the morning Brian puts some food into the Bakery van.

He delivers food to the local school, supermarket and offices in the town.

When he returns he helps Beryl prepare food for lunch time.

They serve lunch in the shop.

The shop closes at two o'clock in the afternoon.

They clean the kitchen and the bakery.

They walk home and they have dinner at five o'clock.

They watch television and they go to bed at half past seven because they get up early.

They work six days a week.

They have Sunday off.

They like their job.

Question.	Answer.
Where do they live?	They live in a small town in Oxfordshire.
What do they do?	They have a Baker's shop.
What time do they get up?	They get up at four o'clock in the morning.
Does Brian bake bread?	Yes, he does.
What time does the shop open?	He opens the shop at seven in the morning.
Does Beryl deliver the food?	No, she does not.
Do they serve lunch in the shop?	Yes, they do.
Do they walk home?	Yes, they do.
Do they work every day?	No, they don't. They have Sunday off.
Do they like their jobs?	Yes, they do.

Thirteen.

We use on for days and dates. On.

Terry and Susan. They are husband and wife.

I go to work on Mondays and I travel on the train.

I visit my Mother on Tuesdays and on Wednesdays I go shopping.

My wife and I play tennis on Thursdays and we finish work early on Fridays.

We drive the car to London on Saturdays. We watch a film and then we book into a hotel.

On Sundays we drive home and then we get ready for the next week.

Days.

What day does he go to work?	He goes to work on Mondays.
What day does he visit his Mother?	He visits his Mother on Tuesdays.
When do they finish work early?	They finish work early on Fridays.
Where do they go on Saturdays?	They go to London on Saturdays.
Where do they go on Sundays?	They drive home.

Dates.

When is New Year's Day?	It is on January 1st.
When is Americas Independence Day?	It is on July 4th.
When is Christmas Day?	It is on December 25th.
When is Boxing Day?	It is on December 26th.
When is your birthday?	It is on………………..

We use at for the exact time.

The Office Worker Dave.

I get up at 7.00 a.m. I have a shower and get ready for work.

I catch the 8.30 a.m. train. It arrives in Manchester at 9.00 a.m.

I start work at 9.30 a.m. I have one hour for lunch at 1.00 p.m.

I finish work at 6.00 p.m. I catch the train home and arrive back at 7.30 p.m.

I watch television and go to bed at 10.30 p.m.

Time.

When does Dave get up?	He gets up at 7.00 a.m.
When does he arrive in Manchester?	He arrives in Manchester at 9.00 a.m.
When does he have lunch?	He has lunch at 1.00 p.m.
When does he arrive home?	He arrives home at 7.30 p.m.
When does he go to bed?	He goes to bed at 10.30 p.m.

We also use at for special occasions like Christmas and Eid.

Children open gifts at Christmas. At Christmas children sing songs and play games.

At Eid people have a party. Parents give children money at Eid.

Special Occasions.

What do children do at Christmas?	They sing songs and play games.
What do people eat at Christmas?	They eat a big dinner.
What do people do at Eid?	They have a party.
Do people have a nice time?	Yes, they do.

When do we use in for months, years and seasons. We use in the for the time of day.

Ryan the school boy.

In winter I wear a hat and coat . I catch the bus to school.

In November, December, January and February it is very cold. In the morning it rains and it is windy.

In summer I wear shorts and a T-Shirt. I walk to school.

In June, July and August it is very warm. In the morning it is hot and in the afternoon it is sunny.

In 2025, I am going to my new school. It is 5 miles from my house so I am going to get up very early and catch a train in the morning to arrive at the school in time.

Months, years, seasons and times of the day.

What does he wear in winter?	He wears a hat and a coat.
What is the weather like in December?	In December it is cold and windy.
What is the weather like in July?	In July it is very warm.
Where is he going in 2025?	He is going to a new school in 2025.

Fourteen.

When do we use and, because, but and so.

We use and for additional information.

I want fish and chips.

We eat fruit and vegetables every day.

I have tea and coffee in the evening.

I sometimes eat bread and butter with salad.

They serve coffee and tea on a plane.

I need pen and paper to write a note.

John and James are twins.

Dave and Anne are getting married next year.

France and Spain are in the European Union.

<u>We use because for the reason we do some thing?</u>

I go to the gymnasium because I want to get fit.

I drink tea because I like it.

We don't eat chocolate because it is bad for you.

They don't have a car because they don't have any money.

He doesn't go to see them because they live in another country.

I drive a car because I like driving.

He works as a teacher because he likes children

He doesn't play football because he hurt his leg.

You don't have a jacket because it is very hot.

You go swimming because it is the best exercise in the water.

When do we use but?

We use but for positive and negative reasons as to why or why not we can do something.

I want to buy a new car but I don't have any money.

1	He likes playing football but he doesn't like watching it.
2	They eat steak but they don't eat fish.
3	My Dad has a car but he doesn't have a bicycle.
4	Jack plays tennis but he doesn't play golf.
5	Frank wants to see his Father this evening but he has to work.
6	Dave and Anne want to come and see us but they are not free next weekend.
7	They are welcome to come to the party but the other people are not.
8	I want to see you but I am too busy at the moment.
9	The cake is delicious, but the sandwiches are terrible.
10	He is a nice man but he wife isn't.

We use so for the reason why we do something?

I want to lose weight so I am going on a diet.

I need to improve my English so I have lessons.
We like dogs so we got one for my Father's birthday.
It is raining so they are taking an umbrella with them.
Harry is feeling ill so he is going to see the Doctor tomorrow.
Jane is tired so she is going to bed early tonight.
We have an important exam next week so we have to study.
He doesn't like his job so he is looking for another one.
She doesn't like the food at that restaurant so she is not going there again.
The cat is so beautiful so we are going to get one..
My family like America so we are going again next year.

Fifteen.

Nations and Nationalities.

Dave a Police Officer.

Question	**Answer**
Where is Dave from?	He is from England. He is English.
Where is Jane from?	She is from Ireland. She is Irish.
Does he speak Spanish?	No, he doesn't.
Does she speak French?	Yes, she does.
Where are they going on holiday?	They are going on holiday to America.

Diane an Air Stewardess.

Question.	Answer.
Where is Diane from?	Diane is from Rome, Italy.
Is she Spanish?	No, she isn't. She is Italian.
Where is she flying to in the evening?	She is flying to Madrid.
Does she speak German?	Yes, she does.
Where is her husband from?	He is from England.

Question.	**Answer.**
Where are Mark and Paul from?	They are from Canada.
What languages does Mark speak?	He speaks English and French.
What languages does Paul speak?	He speaks English, French and Russian.
Where are their passengers from?	They are from France, Canada, Germany, Italy and Poland.
Is the aeroplane Canadian?	No, it is not.
Is the aeroplane American?	Yes, it is.
Are they flying to France this evening?	Yes, they are.
Do they like their jobs?	Yes, they do.

Sixteen

<u>Which of these sports do you play, do or go.</u>

<u>If a sport uses a ball we use the verb to play.</u>

<u>If a sport doesn't use a ball we use the verb to go.</u>

<u>If a sport doesn't use a ball and is usually inside we use do.</u>

Verb	**Sport**
do	athletics
play	basketball
play	cricket
go	diving
do	fencing
play	football
do	gymnastics
play	golf
play	hockey
go	horse riding

go	ice skating
do	judo
do	karate
play	lacrosse
play	netball
play	polo
play	rugby
go	running
go	swimming
play	squash
play	tennis
play	volleyball
do	wrestling
go	yatching
do	yoga

Seventeen.

Adjectives describe places.

Put the adjectives in the correct spaces.

Cairo is an ancient city.

There are lots of historic buildings and it is the home of the ancient pyramids.

It is a very dirty and noisy city.   In the summer it is a very hot place.

International tourists travel to Cairo every year.

hot	old	busy	international	noisy	ancient	historic

Adjectives describe people.

Put the adjectives in the correct spaces.

John is a nice man.

He is a clever person as he works as a Doctor.

He is a hard worker as he works for twelve hours.

He is kind and helpful.

This is what you need to be a good Doctor.

hard	kind	nice	good	helpful	clever

Adjectives describe things.

Put the adjectives in the correct spaces.

I have a new computer.

The computer is nice and fantastic.

It is an expensive computer.

expensive	new	fantastic	nice	great

Eighteen.

Comparative and Superlative Adjectives.

Remember the adjectives describe the nouns.

Rule One.

For some comparative and superlatives we add -er and -est.

tall
old
young
small
kind

tall.

The Empire State is a	tall	building.
The Sears Tower is	taller	than the Empire State.
The Burja Khalifa is the	tallest	building in the world.

old.

Rome is an	old	city.
Athens is	older	than Rome.
Luxor is the	oldest	city in the world.

young.

A child is a	young	person.
A infant is	younger	than a child.
A baby is	the	youngest.

small.

A cat is a	small	animal.
A mouse is	smaller	than a cat.
An insect is	the	smallest.

kind.

Peter a	kind	man.
Tony is	kinder	than Peter.
Dennis is the	kindest	man.

We add -er and -est to these adjectives.

Remember Comparatives compare two sets of things and Superlative look at three sets of things.

Rule Two.

If adjective ends in y we drop the y and add -ier and -iest.

funny

lazy

busy

noisy

happy

funny.

Jimmy is a	funny	man.
John is	funnier	than Jimmy.
Gerry is the	funniest	person in the family.

lazy.

Andy is a	lazy	man.
Chris is	lazier	than Andy.
Eddie is the	laziest	laziest person in the group.

busy.

Manchester is a	busy	city.
London is	busier	than Manchester.
Tokyo is the	busiest	city in the world.

noisy.

Delhi is a	noisy	city.
Paris is	noisier	than Delhi.
Cairo is the	noisiest	city in the world.

happy.

Adele is a	happy	child.
Melanie is	happier	than Adele.
Alison is the	happiest	person in the group.

This rule also applies to adjectives like crazy, dirty and easy.

Rule Three.

Some adjectives follow more with the adjective and the most with the adjective.

beautiful

dangerous

expensive

important

responsible

beautiful.

A Ford is a	beautiful	car.
A Porsche is	more beautiful	than a Ford.
A Rolls Royce is	the most beautiful	car.

Dangerous.

Polar Bears are	dangerous	animals.
Snakes are	more dangerous	than Polar Bears.
Lions are the	most dangerous	animals.

expensive.

It is an	expensive	silver ring.
The gold ring is	more expensive	than the silver ring.
The Diamonds are	the most expensive	things.

important.

A private is an	important	soldier.
An officer is	more important	than a soldier.
A General is the	most important	soldier.

responsible.

A teacher is a	responsible	person.
A senior teacher is	more responsible	than a teacher.
A Headteacher is the	most responsible	person in a school.

Remember for this rule we use more

adjective

the most   adjective.

Rule Four

Irregular Adjectives.

A few adjectives do not follow these rules.

They are good, bad, many and little.

good	better	the best
bad	worse	the worst
many	more	the most.
little	less	the least.

Good

David is a	good	footballer.
Mark is a	better footballer	than David.
Peter is the	best	footballer on the team.

Bad

It is	bad	weather today in England.
In Scotland it is	worse	than England.
Ireland has the	worst	weather today.

Many

There are	many	tables in the class.
There are	more	tables in the next class.
There are the	most	tables in the storeroom.

<u>Little.</u>

There is a	little	petrol in my car.
There is	less	petrol in Dave's car.
There is the	least	petrol in Mark's car.

<u>Twenty.</u>

<u>English Games.</u>

Count to a hundred and you can say a hundred words in English in under a minute without the letter a in it.

What starts with T ends with T and is full of T?

Teapot.

Can you name me five English Semi-Professional or Professional Football Teams that start and end with the same letter?

Aston Villa, Chartlon Athletic, Liverpool, Northampton Town and York City.

Printed in Great Britain
by Amazon

81780937R00066